# Wilderness of Ladies

# ELEANOR ROSS TAYLOR

# Wilderness of Ladies

### With an Introduction
### by RANDALL JARRELL

*With Best Wishes,*
*Eleanor Ross Taylor*

## McDOWELL, OBOLENSKY
### New York

"Moved," "At the Carnival," and "Family Bible" have appeared in *Botteghe Oscure*; "Playing" in *The Virginia Quarterly Review*; "Sister and "The Bine Yadkin Rose" in *Poetry Magazine*; "Wind," "Goodbye Family," "Buck Duke and Mamma," "Woman as Artist," and "Flesh and Spirit" in *Accent*.

Manufactured in the United States of America by
The Haddon Craftsmen, Scranton, Pennsylvania.

# Contents

For Peter

# Introduction

Buck Duke says to Mamma, as he brings her the milk-pail full of wild plums:

"Sour! Your eyes'll water, Miss Tempe!
But sweet, too."

The taste of someone else's life—and while you are reading these poems you are someone else—is almost too sour to be borne; but sweet, too. The life is that of one woman, one (as the census would say) housewife; but a family and section and century are part of it, so that the poems have the "weight and power,/ Power growing under weight" of a world. Some of this world is grotesquely and matter-of-factly funny, some of it is tragic or insanely awful—unbearable, one would say, except that it is being borne. But all of it is *so*, seen as no one else could see it, told as no one else could tell it.

The poems and poet come out of the Puritan South. This Scotch Presbyterianism translated into the wilderness is, for her, only the fierce shell of its old self, but it is as forbidding and compulsive as ever: the spirit still makes its unforgiving demands on a flesh that is already too weak to have much chance in the struggle. The things of this world are "what Ma called poison lilies, sprouting/ From Back Bunn's meadow resurrectionwise/ But with a sinful pink stain at the throat." So much, still, is sin! Blaming the declining West, a character in one of the poems says hotly: "You talk so much of rights, now;/ You ask so seldom what your duties are!" The poet knows too well for asking what her duties are, and has no rights except the right to do right and resent it: her "Lord, help me to be more humble in this world!" is followed without a pause by the exultant "In that Great, Getting-up Morning, there will be another song!" She cannot permit herself—the whole life she has inherited will not permit her—to be happy, innocently bad, free of these endless demands, this continual self-condemnation. Frost speaks of a world where work is "play for mortal stakes," but here everything is work for mortal stakes, and harder because of the memory of play, now that nothing is play. (I once heard a woman say, about buying new clothes for a trip to Europe: "It's work, Mary, it's work!"—a very Protestant and very ethical sentence.) First there were her own family's demands on the girl, and now there are the second family's demands on the woman; and worst of all, hardest of all, are the woman's demands on herself—so that sometimes she longs to be able to return to the demands of the first family, when the immediate world was at least childish and natural, and one still had child allies in the war against the grown-ups. Now the family inside, the conscience, the superego, is a separate, condemning self from which there is no escape except in suicide or fantasies of suicide, the dark rushing not-I into which the I vanishes. And which, really, is the I? The demanding conscience, or the part that tries to meet—tries, even, to escape from —its demands? In one poem the chain gang guard envies the prisoner who still needs a guard, who cannot escape because of the rifle outside, the guard outside; the guard himself no longer has to be guarded, says in despairing mockery: "As if I'd get away!" The world is a cage for a woman, and inside it the woman is her own cage. In longing regression, this divided self—"riding the trolley homeward this afternoon/ With the errands in my lap"—would have "disfestooned my world—/ A husband, more or less!/A family, more or less!— To have alighted to a cup of kettle-tea/ And someone/ To whom I could lie merrily,/ Use malapropisms, be out-of-taste"; to the sister who is "more than one-flesh-and-blood,/ Almost one I." The self, two now, longs for that first world in which it and another were, almost, one; longs to return to the make-believe tea that preceded the real tea of the grown-ups, the tea that, drunk, makes one a wife and mother.

The world of the poems is as dualistic as that of Freud; everything splits, necessarily, into two warring opposites. This fault along which life divides, along which the earthquakes of existence occur, is for the poet primal—underlies all the gaps, disparities, cleavages, discontinuities that run right through her; she could say with Emerson, "There is a crack in everything that God has made." She says about her sister and herself, "The wars of marriage and the family burst around us"—but these are only external duplicates of the war inside, the war of self

6

and self. Life is a state of siege, of desperate measures, forlorn hopes, last extremities—is war to the last woman. Carried far enough, anything reduces to a desperate absurdity; one can say about the poems themselves what one of them says about a man: "You were a mortal sheen/ Flickering from the negative." The poems' Religious Wars, wars of conscience, go over into wars of anxiety and anguish, of neurosis or psychosis: "For me the expected step sinks,/ The expected light winks/ Out . . ." The water of sexuality, of unknown experience, that the child shrank from and that the woman longs to drown in, freezes into glass, gems, the hard "stock-dead" fixity of catatonia:

> Oh to have turned at the landing
> And never have sounded the bell
> That somehow thrust me in this room
> Beaded with eyes, painfully held
> To the liable frame I illume.
> Could life stop, or go on!
> But olives dangle crystal stems,
> And that clock muffles its French tick
> In those elaborate kiss-me-knots;
> Does it, too, hate its gems?

In frigid aberration, she spoils the life she ought to nourish: "Each year I dug and moved the peonies/ Longing to flare/ Fat and chemically by the well-slab,/ Ingrown./ Every day I opened the drawer and/ Scanned the knives"; and the warped spirit (after it has desperately demanded, from outside, the miracle that alone could have saved it: "You should have struck a light/ In the dark I was, and/ Said, Read, Be—be over!") ends in an awful negative apotheosis, as it cries: "Not in the day time, not in the dark time/ Will my voice cut and my poison puff/ My treasures of flesh,/ My gems of flashing translucent spirit,/ Nor my caress shatter them." When, in one poem, a patient says, "It nettled me to have them touch my dog/ And say in their dispelling voices, Dog," the helpless, fretful, loving-its-own-neurosis voice of the neurotic is so human that your heart goes out to it, and can neither pigeonhole it nor explain it away.

The violent emotion of so much of the poetry would be in-

7

tolerable except for the calm matter-of-factness, the seriousness and plain truth, of so much else; and except for the fact that this despairing extremity is resisted by her, forced from her, instead of being exaggerated for effect, depended on as rhetoric, welcomed for its own sake, as it is in that existential, beatnik Grand Guignol that is endemic in our age. And, too, there is so much that is funny or touching, there are so many of the homely, natural beauties known only to someone "who used to notice such things." How much of the old America is alive in lines like "She took a galloping consumption/ After she let the baby catch on fire . . ./ And Cousin Mazeppa took laudanum./ 'Why did you do it, Zeppie girl?/ Wa'n't Daddy good to you?'/ 'Pray, let me sleep!' "—Byron and Liszt and Modjeska end at this country crossroads, in a name. How could old-maidly, maiden-ladyish refinement be embodied more succinctly, funnily, and finally than in:

> *Miss Bine taught one to violet the wrists.*
> *"I accuse you, Mr. Stapleton,*
> *Of excess temperance—ha ha!"*
> *"Miss Tempe. . . . I beg. . . . Allow me to insist—!"*?

The old woman, dying among images, sees out on the dark river of death, past Cluster Rocks, "an old lady her uncles rowed across—/ The boat beneath her slipped the bank/ Just as she stepped ashore./ 'Stretched me arightsmart,' she chirped./ O to think of that dying!/ O unworthy 'Stretchedmearightsmart'!/ She glared at hell through tears." This country humor, that comes out of a natural knowledge like that of Hardy or Faulkner, can change into a gallows-humor that once or twice has the exact sound and feel of Corbière: the suicide on her way into the water mutters, "It's no good God's whistling, 'Come back, Fido' "; the cold benighted lovers flee down the blocked-off "last bat-out-of-hell roads:/ *Closed, Under Destruction.*" But these and other humors—the humors of dreams, of neurosis, of prosaic actuality —all come together in a kind of personal, reckless charm, an absolute individuality, that make one remember Goethe's "In every artist there is a germ of recklessness without which talent is inconceivable."

8

In the beginning there were no ladies in the wilderness, only squaws. These were replaced, some generations ago, by beings who once, in another life, were ladies; once were Europeans. To these lady-like women in the wilderness there is something precious and unnatural about lady-likeness, about the cultivated European rose grafted upon the wild American stem. But "pretense had always been their aim," even in childhood; their conscious female end is that genteel, cultured, feminist old-maidishness that—intact, thorny, precisely self-contained—rises above the masculine, disreputable economic and sexual necessity that reaches out to strip off their blossoms, that makes you "dish potatoes up three times a day,/ And put your wedding dress into a quilt," that turns young ladies into old women. This Victorian old-maidish culture has its continuation in the *House Beautiful, Vogue*-ish sophistication that the poet calls "Our exotic properties, our pretty price./ The garden radish lies on ice, the radish rose./ Smordgasbord!" The new *déjeuner sur l'herbe* is summed up, bitterly, in the old terms, the plain, religious, country terms: "Dinner on the grounds! and the blessing still unsaid . . ." The poet looks askance at this acquired surface, even in herself— especially in herself, since it belongs neither to her wild heart nor her neo-Calvinist conscience. To her there is something natural and endearing about the crushing wilderness, the homely childish beauties that one relaxes or regresses into. It is the ladies who are really barren, so that one might say: *You make a desert and call her a lady*; and in what is perhaps the most beautiful and touching of all these poems, *Buck Duke and Mamma,* it is human feeling, natural sexuality, that the girl at last accepts in grief, and it is the histrionic feminine gentility that she rejects.

If these poems are less about the New Woman than about the Old (surviving, astonished, into this age of appliances and gracious fun), still, no poems can tell you better what it is like to be a woman; none come more naturally out of a woman's ordinary existence, take both their subjects and their images out of the daily and nightly texture of her life. Many of these are what I think of as woman's-work-is-never-done images: cooking, sewing, ironing, taking care of children, tending the sick, and so on; but these pass, through gardening, on over into the lady-like images of social existence, distrusted things akin to all the images of glass, mirrors, gems of coldness, hardness, and dryness of two-ness, cleavages, opposites, negatives, of trapped circular motion, that express a range of being from gentility to catatonia. These are lightened, colored, by images from childhood and the past—counting-out rhymes, hymns, slave-songs, and so on. A pervading, obsessive image is that of light in darkness: there are so many stars, meteors, flames, snowflakes, feathers, that one almost feels that the poems themselves can be summed up in the sentence in which the dying old woman sums up her life: "My quick, half-lighted shower, are you gone?" Often these images merge with the ruling, final image of the poems, that of water: the water of experience or sexuality, into which the little girl is afraid to wade; the river the dying woman remembers from childhood and must cross, now, into the next world; life's dark star-bearing flood trapped in the mill of daily duties, of reduced mechanical existence: "The water pushes the mill wheel;/ The wheel, wheeling, dispersing,/ Disperses the starry spectacle/ And drags the stone"—or frozen into the fixity of glass, mirrors, the hateful gems that send the hands on in their aimless endless circle. Even love or sexuality is seen in terms of water freezing into, or melting among the "thin floes," the cold clandestine darkness of a country night. You destroy yourself, escape from yourself, in water: in *Goodbye Family,* "under the foundations of God's world/ Lilily/ Swimming on my side" until at last "the water/ Meeting me around the curve, roaring, blanks/ Out all"; and in *Escape,* as "a vein of time gapes for her small transfusion," disappearing into the ocean with a "far white crash too negligible to bear." "Art and death" are "both oceans on my map," the map of the *Woman as Artist,* woman as lover. And woman ends, man ends, "Lying at the edge of the water," face in the water: "when our faces are swol up/ We will look strange to them./ Nobody, looking out the door/ Will think to call us in./ They'll snap their fingers trying/ To recollect our names"; the rope is broken, no one ever again will draw up the bucket bobbing at the bottom of the well of death. In the poems everything goes together, everything has several reasons for being what it is: the whole book is, so to speak, one dream, that expresses with extraordinary completeness and finality the life of the dreamer.

Many of the poems show (rather as the end of *The Old Wives' Tale* shows) what you might call human entropy—life's residual reality, what is so whatever else is so. That life, just lived, is death; that its first pure rapturous flame grows greater, fouls itself, diminishes, struggles and goes out: the poems say it with terrible magic:

> *In the morning, early,*
> *Birds flew over the stable,*
> *The morning glories ringed the flapping corn*
> *With Saturn faces for the surly light*
> *And stars hung on the elder night.*

But soon the sun is gone, the stars go out as the old woman's eyes close. Life is a short process soon over: how quickly the lyric, girlish, old-fashioned funniness of *My Grandmother's Virginhood, 1870* becomes the worn, sad grown-upness of *Motherhood, 1880!*—the girl's kiss so soon is the woman's sick or dying baby, her eroded featureless "They know I favor this least child."

The poems are full of personal force, personal truth—the first and last thing a reader sees in a writer—down to the least piece of wording. Their originality is so entire, yet so entirely natural, that it seems something their writer deserves no credit for: she could do no other. Just as the poems' content ranges from pure fact to pure imagination, so their language ranges from a folk speech as authentically delightful as Hardy's or Faulkner's (though the poet's use of folk material reminds me even more of Janacek's and Bartok's) to a poetic style so individual that you ask in wonder: How can anything be so queer and yet so matter-of-fact—natural, really? Picasso has said that when you find the thing yourself it is always ugly, the others after you can make it beautiful. Sometimes this is true of these poems; and yet sometimes she has found it beautiful, or has made it into a marvel you don't call either beautiful or ugly—have no words for:

> *Was it forgiven? It was gone,*
> *The heathen dancing*

*With her giggling sisters;*
*They flew about the room*
*In seedstitch weskits*
*Like eight wax dolls gone flaskwards.*
*Those were gay days!*
*She sighed a mournful tune*
*Waddling about her everyday*
*Affairs of life and death*
*(Affairs of painful life, uncertain death):*
*"Wild loneliness that beats*
*Its wings on life," she sang.*
*She thwacked a pone in two,*
*Her big hand for a knife.*
*Thar! stirring it severely,*
*And thar! into the oven . . .*

There is plenty of detached objective observation in the poems, but usually they are objective in another sense: they are so much the direct expression of the object that their words are still shaking with it—are, so to speak, *res gestae,* words that, repeated, are not hearsay evidence but part of the fact itself. The poet continually makes a kind of inevitable exclamation, has wrenched from her a law or aphorism, a summing-up, that is at the same time an animal cry. Sometimes her speech is the last speech before speechless desperation—too low to be heard as sound, only felt as pain; but sometimes it is like sunlight on fall leaves, firelight on cornbread. The book presents as they have never been presented before—which is to say, as every true artist has presented them—our everyday affairs of life and death.

Some of the very best of these poems, I think, are *Buck Duke and Mamma, Song, Woman as Artist, Moved, Family Bible* (especially *Grandparents*), *The Bine Yadkin Rose,* and *Goodbye Family;* poems like *Madame, In the Churchyard, The Chain Gang Guard,* and *Playing* are slighter or smaller, but realized past change. Readers who know the poems well will feel an impatient disgust at me for some of the poems I haven't named, the qualities I haven't mentioned. And all the poems are far more than the best poems: the pieces, put together, are a world.

When one reads poems here and there, in magazines and manuscript, it seems very unlikely that they should be good almost as Dickinson's or Hardy's poems are. Of course the readers who first saw Dickinson's and Hardy's poems, in magazines and manuscripts, thought it just as unlikely that the poems should be good almost as Wordsworth's were. The readers knew what the poems weren't, what the poems couldn't be; and because of this it was hard for them to see what the poems were. An introduction to a book like *Wilderness of Ladies* might make it easier for readers to consider the possibility of the poems' being what they are.

Randall Jarrell

# The Bine Yadkin Rose

Bemiracled rose, I see my cutting took:
Sad horn, the spell-rocked cradle of a rose—
Look! how the foster brier grows
That mother bed, that lover bed forsook

Miss Tempe went to sew for Miss Bine
Before she ever thought of being Mamma,
The smoothing, the whistling, a scissorly-wise drama,
Her life a raggy scrapbag pantomime.
    (The artful rose of stiff, dispiteous stem
    Blenched lest a natural beauty should offend.)

Miss Bine taught one to violet the wrists.
'I accuse you, Mr. Stapleton,
Of excess temperance—ha-ha!"
"Miss Tempe. . . . I beg. . . . Allow me to insist—!"

In autumn near dusk a bad cloud came up.
The heavens turned drear, Miss Bine turned white.
'I fear God is near," she croaked. "Let's light a light."
They set a fiery candle in a teacup.
    (The spicy daughters of rank greenhouse whims
    Blench lest a natural vanity offend.)

Unringed, but wed, she took a ring and wed unwed,
A bouquet of pink hyacinths at her waist.
Her thumping heart denied her chilling taste
But well believed the deadly words she said.

Move into a house that's not yet built,
And there's scant time to prune a rose and spray.
You dish potatoes up three times a day,
And put your wedding dress into a quilt.
    (The chary husband stiff dispity wins
    Quails lest uxorial charity set in.)

Pray let me not unduly understand
This ring-a-rosy of our distant hands,

Nor color up, just barely cultivate;
An austere blossom for each Sunday plate,

For a sisterhood in multiple rosettes,
Adoring our Victorian regrets.

# Moved

No more carting in or out or off,
No more saying old or new; instead
We'll dust the smiles that are discovered:
All is distributed.
Today for the first time
Mrs. Presterling revised
A spontaneity; I dropped my eyes.

Last things close in upon us
Like storm windows hung a week too soon.
Between the mullions I stare out into
The placid incubator where
Other life, somehow, cares to move.

To this address they will come,
All the bad news of losses that must be.
To this we desolate will come,
Older, from our other homes.
And I know certainly now, come or not,
Our line-oak softened at the core with rot,
The woods grown deeper so that simple light
Falling across the path perplexes sight,
The houses frailer and an ell, a porch,
Drawn off in chains behind a tractor,
The tractor back to smooth the pitching hills,
Our garden hung with hardening gourds,
A spot where idle birds whet idle bills.

And Mrs. Presterling, sweet heartsbane still
But gone drawn white and pinched, at our back door
Holding a coat together at her throat
With long blue fingers; rapidly and loudly:
"My husband's fallen, and I think he's dead."
She does not know whether to hurry, or
To stop on the path by the pitcher bed.

And we will languish idly in the yard-chairs.
How strange the shadows of the chickens are!
Because the sun is changing at this time, my dear;
In an hour or so all will be dark.
And there will be the spot upon the table
Where you or I set our last medicine glass,
As if a clapperless glass bell
Were covered by another, were covered by another,
Covered by a larger, clear
Glass bell.
Will there not be liftings-up?
Will there not be lazy breakfasts, with friends?
Will there be births in spiraling gardens?
Yes yes, but this is of ends.

# Playing

In Ugly Creek they dashed their toes.
The Cyril Mabry cows arose
And water spiders stepped aside
To watch how little girls would wade;
A summer picnic well delayed
Might miss the churn-turned fireside.

Those old folks always have been old. . .
Those childhoods tell-re-over-told
Are just a pocket full of seeds
That never generated weeds. . . .

When the little girls returned to the bank
Their little fingers swelled and shrank!
A frigid, leafless shadow lay
Upon the water-throated day.
They piled their hands to play a game—
Pretense had always been their aim. . . .
What was it, little girls became?
Take it off, knock it off, or
Have the crows peck it off—?
The little hands . . . they somehow shake;
The little bones they somehow quake.

Where's my share? Cat got it.
Where's cat? In the woods.
Where's woods? Water squenched.
Where's ox? Rope lynched.
Where's rope? "Dead and buried
Behind the new church door
And the first that laughs or grins or shows
His teeth
Gets a slap, and a kick, and a knock, and a—
Wreath."

The female bitter black tongues hum
The palms forsake the stiffened thumb
(The waiting womb! the waiting tomb—
The empty antique sitting room!)
Before the final griefs succumb—

ROBERT, YOU LEFT OUT SOME!
You left out some!
You left out some!
Watt . . . left out some. . . .

# Wind

From the moment Gabriella died
At an exhausted, nightless morning time
A knifestruck disattendance cast a gloom
In any place she might have chanced to be,
Even in places properly mine—
In my bedroom, at my fireside—
That made me rise at once and leave a room
Instantly her formal blank came in to me;
The one last-minute, dry-pen silence drew
A grave, regretful, canceling line through
All my blotted teas. There was nothing to say
And it was no use looking for anything,
In the cupboards, or out the door.
Long ago, something had eaten out my marrow,
And I was hungry now, for years before.

My flaxseed-meal aunts touched my arm:
"Faith holds no room for such alarm—"
But the wind of a suddenly-turned season,
Hard, and raw enough to move a solid shadow,
Began in flaws to rush the outer closures
And wheedle through the inner apertures,
Calling together broken flowered cups,
Uncommunicative inked-out reasons,
Recalling losses that had hinged
On cheese toast and the cats' piece-meals;
I even felt my cradle agonies
Alone, in the dark back room, revealed
In the wind fighting the oaks, seizing life
Just so. In the wind's seizure I saw her
Trudging barefoot and mudfouled
Over the clay with strength grown bodywise,
And wherever the dreamy, cultivated
Part of her had fled to—
It was not in her ghost, nervous, human eyes
I kept seeing.
                        Gabriella, howl!

## Sister

And we two alone here in this peace pan
Are ever strolling uphill to the old-house-place;
The path washed out, grown up, but not erased:
The wars of marriage and the family burst around us.

When I was young, folks thought me pretty.
I took my charms up to the city. . . .
I didn't like it there.
Oh, the poems Mamma burned in those days!
*You* made Mamma cry. Her tears fell in the dough. . .
I'm not well, that's why. I told you so.
Why did you go and have me? I hate you all.
Lord, help me to be more humble in this world.
(Don't tell on me. I hid the pieces in the dungeon.)
Lord, help me to be more humble in this world!
In that Great, Getting-up Morning, there will be an-
other song!

In the old-house there was cotton,
Piled shoulder high to climb on,
Soundless and seedy—exotic,
And the floor smelled seasonround of guano.
We walked about and about the house at night.
Hear the frogs creak in the pasture! (I thought
The stars made that noise when they came out)
No! no! no! no! my dear!

Then we discovered within the close
Our exotic properties, our pretty price.
The garden radish lies on ice, the radish rose.
Smordgasbord! and the 'Venerable
Silver-throated horn' unsounded;
Dinner on the grounds! and the blessing still unsaid;
The sun that baked our mud-bread
Hides slyly in the trees

Between Spring Garden and Milton Streets
And howls at what we eat.

And riding the trolley homeward this afternoon
With the errands in my lap
I would have disfestooned my world—
A husband, more or less!
A family, more or less!—
To have alighted to a cup of kettle-tea
And someone
To whom I could lie merrily,
Use malapropisms, be out-of-taste,
Without regretting that old warfare waste,
Without acknowledging the sib discard—
Black king, black jack, black heart;
We'd play it solitary while the dusks rushed by,
More than one-flesh-and-blood,
Almost one I.

# Goodbye Family

The sounds I hear from the evening chambers
    Stanch my breath.
Whether I sit alone in the parlor
    Or whether
Ladies crack nuts and ice cubes there, I hear
    Tiptoeing,
A banging head, and breath stops for fear
    Of what I am doing there
Clanging and pacing in the rooms
    Of next year.
For hate-you paralyzed my lover's shrug;
    My stare
Froze down the only warmth another had,
    All her own;
Each year I dug and moved the peonies
    Longing to flare
Fat and chemically by the well-slab,
    Ingrown.
Every day I opened the drawer and
    Scanned the knives;
Were there enough, sharp enough,
    For all lives?

The years to climb! The walls to catch at!
    To cut free
And drop through the cloak closet and cellar
    Is better—
Under the foundations of God's world
    Lilily
Swimming on my side, with ear on shoulder,
    Eyes unlettered,
And intellectuality an asterisk
    Now blurred—
It's no use God's whistling, "Come back, Fido,
    "Come back,

"I won't tease any more." I'm in the glade
    Remembering
I meant to tell my daughter, "I looked for
    You a cattail
But they were all silked out"—
    And now the water
Meeting me around the curve, roaring, blanks
    Out all but ear:
        Not in the day time, not in the dark time
        Will my voice cut and my poison puff
        My treasures of flesh
        My gems of flashing translucent spirit,
        Nor my caress shatter them.

# Buck Duke and Mamma

He came bringing us a milkpail full
Of speckled, wild, goose plums—
All fat unsmelt-out perfumedom—
And perched on the back porch curb to taste a few.
"Sour! Your eyes'll water, Miss Tempe!
But sweet, too."
Mamma's way was posing by the silent pool
And tossing in the line amiss
That shook the skies of the other world
And all but loosed the roots of this.
She trimmed and trained the roundabout backwoods,
Was glad that Buck Duke had a devilish eye;
It saved an orphan from dire fortitude,
And saved his grandpa's house from sanctity.
"Your Papa doesn't favor your going there.
I say, enter evil to cure evil, if you dare!"
As she went about her cast-off household chores
She overlooked them with a lavish bow
Inspired by that heroine of poems,
Her elocution teacher, Miss Hattie Yow.
    "Nothing to do? In this world of ours?
    Where weeds spring daily amidst sweet flowers?"
    Your-mammy-never-came-to-much-my-Buck.

"Don't drink that Mackling Spring's brack water
Whe'r it's high or low.
The cows stand in there and let go."
But old Duke's beardy words were moss for campfire
When they took their kitchen rations to the woods.
Mamma's boys looked out for sassafras, but Buck
Made frog gigs, thrashed Mackling Spring into a suds.
("I say, dear boys! Be good. Take care.
But learn a little evil! if you dare. . . .")
His thirst once drunk, turned drunken,
And Buck Duke tossed all night, all day,

Made rusty speeches on old swapping knives,
Called names that paled the sallow-boned herbwives,
Tore off the sleeping clothes, his bed's, his own,
And never seemed to wake.
His boyish modesty ran dry,
At last the hands cooled, then the face.
Mamma stood at his bedside.
She overlooked him with a sprightly brow
Inspired by that gay mistress of mad poesy
Her elocution teacher, Miss Hattie Yow.
    " 'Stop stop pretty waters' cried Mary one day
        'My vessel, my flowers you carry away.' "

Mamma made a wreath of all her flowers:
The histrionic garden did not bear
One saucy pose when she put down the scissors;
The battered bees hung stupid in mid-air.
She worked on knees and elbows on the back porch,
That savage zinnia ornament compiled,
Then all at once cooped up her face
With hands like bird's wings—
A gesture, she knew, would have made Miss Hattie smile.

# Cleavage

When those big eyes came down on mine
Across the room, I knew my time
Had come. Must I speak now—or wait?
Oh the brave wranglers gone before!
Did none find out a sweet side door
Opening on a terrace sunbound
In all weathers?

Oh to have turned at the landing
And never have sounded the bell
That somehow thrust me in this room
Beaded with eyes, painfully held
To the liable frame I illume.
Could life stop, or go on!
But olives dangle crystal stems,
And that clock muffles its French tick
In those elaborate kiss-me-knots;
Does it, too, hate its gems?

I grasp the group and pull them near—
They seem to see, they seem to hear;
But she—she—
How she stares!
Bemusedly, to crack the whip. . . .
If we could only drop it here,
Nor ever have to have it out. . . .
"My soul," letting her hair drip
A way I find I care about,
"You did your best to salvage us?"
Wild mirrored image, what's left to discuss?
You've told me nothing wholly right.
Mere eyes, I see, have no insight.
"Pull down 'your' hat, pull back 'your' hair"—
Who cares about *your* last dumb breath of air?
      The whole raw showdown comes on drunkenly.

## Cousin Ida

She waked to snow,
And let the morning go,
For she was old.

That hushed onset
Comes but to blank
My distant, might-be-yet world, too,
All worlds, all peep shows in all eggs.

On the piazza, from east edge sunburnt
To west edge burnt, our voiles still warm
From the iron, we rocked, our passage learnt,
Hemstitching and featherstitching, charmed
Yet sighing, that heat and light went hand in glove.
We prepared for marriage, or—rather—love.

One night he'd had a drop too much (my beau
Smiled gently but was not a gentleman)
Snored by the parlor fire and scorched his toe.
They found that highly entertaining.
But while I was gone off to Beulah Springs
They cut my wedding dress to jabots
And I came back without a ring or hope.
(How droll of me to love a parlor joke!)

Flora, Ida, Tempe—Tempe wryly
The day black Uncle Wylie died:
"Good-bye-sir, Wylie!
"You ought t've been gone from here long ago!"
We took him figs and tea a year;
He kept his shoulder to the wheel of death.
We never combed our hair ourselves
Till we were twenty, and Tempe said,
"It tires one so, combing one's hair;
"I give out in my shoulders;

"Let's do each other's now."
But Ida rising from her vanity—
"Not I! We should've been gone from here long ago."

About my shoulders now the snow
That was a fall of stars. . . .
    When the stars fell it was unearthly bright;
    We read unwritten texts by that sharp light.
    "More rain, more rest—"
        "What's that you say?"
    "Master, more rain, more grass!"
    World's coming to an end.
    And Guinea, that's gone, too,
    Cold sparks just out of reach.
Afterwards, the night was dark; wind rose,
A smoky wind, and I waked
Listening, twice towards dawn,
To see if the world went on.

Does this hushed onset come to blank
My distant, might-be-yet world, too?

I, captive, cage-fond,
Dread doors opening on the great beyond.
That bird they said had no song of her own
Cries from the black gum to my ears alone
The very sentence she would say when I was four.
You leave me untranslated, wife of snow!
But now it's grown midnight.
Don't scream for glossaries.
Sh, bird. Let's sleep.
Within our feathered wings,
Within our snow.

One year I clapped my hand over my eyes
When spring came, and when I took it down
My knuckles were speckled brown.
In the middles, in the red cotton bloom,
Each warm clod with its darker side,
Its sprouting seeds of the staved-off jungle,
Slaves still sang:
*Tiding down the backband, tiding down the bow
Tiding down the backband, who made the bow?*

Not I! Good-bye-sir-Wylie!
We should've been gone from here long ago!
God made the bow.

They bound me up in ribbons, moiré bows,
My hair so tight it left no play for face,
My waist so tight it left no space for plea.
"Child, you'll be miserable," they warned, "Don't go."
(Stay here where suffering's homemade, sure to fit.)
Mine never has worn out, though it's grown thin
Now, like a veil. I see through it
When the shadows are right. Light dwindles
In the outer world, and my own ember,
Knocked about like a goody in a nut,
Shines smally through—dormant—convoluted—
Half a notion to spill out.
The deaths of my sisters seems known
To me already; soon, my own;
Chill comes and goes; warm life's phenomenon.
I find myself waking in the night,
Listening to see if the world goes on.
My quick, half-lighted shower, are you gone?

# At the Carnival

At the carnival she told the hands.
A moment left her with her own outfanned,
Her worn heart lines maze-fallen into place,
A crow's foot one finger could unlace
No loop of.
      (Now for the heart of the matter. . . .
      Don't strip the heart. That's loot unspilt,
      The snapped-to locket, like an embryo
      Etched with inheritance and fate—

      A fatal two,
      Swifting it along the king's highway
      At free close kinless tilt,
      When trucks jeered past
      Protecting each other
      Like old mother and son
      Or grandfather and daughter;
      The numb lights lingered on our motley coats;
      The sand grains clung together in thin floes.
      Hedges and white sand roads froze,
      That hardest winter,
      And never came again—
      Blocked off, the last bat-out-of-hell roads:
      *Closed, Under Destruction:*
      One night so dark the eyesight shivered,
      As if a darkness snowed,
      Then one so bright the stars
      Their white leached out, hung glintless pastes;
      Not night, not day, some other tell of time,
      Some other time so fast our stops seemed haste.
      It was so cold we could only hope to hurt each other;
      Never were hands gripped harder;
      Two, skirting light and faced
      With the indicative gullets of a farmer's dogs—
      "Never let it be said we led a chase. . . .

Drop flat."
A liking for the black that darked out names,
But shame for anything like shame,
Rage for a scant publicity of flares, or flags—
Bad waters licked under the cruiseways frozen over,
Cornstalks like catscratch harassed my witch's garb
        "Those one-eyed rabbits, loping, slow. . . ."
        "Give them the slip? They're in the know. . . .
        What do they know? A sneaking might—
        A fool contraption with double sight."
Love-words fell numb, they whispered out, one burst,
And a mist settled no growth could overgrow.
That bracelet I lost there, I'd prize the price of now.
    Its faint sapphire might break the ice fire's hanging in—)
Eyes, don't beseech her so!

# A While Absented

This is a page it's difficult to turn,
Knowing tomorrow there's no looking back;
A page impossible to learn
Now that tomorrow's come.
Here every leaf of Gambier Street
Casts an obscuring shade
On love's ghost balconies
Till the mills pluck down to maple bones—
The villas stand complete—
And the year's come.
But God, age-napping now and then
Lets fall a day of winter time in May;
The flowered white spireas burn,
And spring is ruined.
And the year's ruined.
And many a life's ruined, too.
What can I do
But mark our place
Since there's no reading more?

# The Chain Gang Guard

The pick strikes differently on the rock
And some resists and some dislodges.
The cars that pass us eye us curiously—
Stodged with our eyes, our frozen triggers cocked.
They move free enough; for them, they're jolly—
The blonde one, swinging, sings, "Just like a tree,
Just like a tree, planted by the waters,
I shall not be moved." Easy to see
His spirit's not yet broken. That first chow—
Nose took a squint and stomach shut its eyes;
"I can't eat that," he said. The others spat.
"You may think you can't, but, brother, you lie!"

I don't dare glance to hail the folks I know.
He'll curse or laugh or both as he sees fit,
Cry out to give a stranger's ears a whack,
And throw his hat up for a powdered nose,
Baby oh baby oh baby her,
Die to know where she's off-to up the road.
Playmate, you aint going nowheres
Unless you want to hear my gun unload.

If I had ever learned to tear-up-jack,
Got drunk enough to leave myself behind,
Could know which time to take and which to pay—
Here I stand! loaded gun across me—
As if I'd get away!

## Knives and Forks

The foreign tablecloth was mazed with cutwork;
Vestigial candles shadowed the buffet,
Leapt, fired, between the faces;
Plates, many empty plates,
Continually were removed and set again. . . .
Let them wait.
All trappings currently civilized in dress,
(Merci mille fois—those proper advances!
Sir, if that had been a passionate speech
Not even I could have come between us and him)
Forced ice in glasses to resist forced heat,
(Further, sir, had it been a devoted speech)
The question boomerang that each
Invented for his wise demur—
There as expected. (And lastly, sir—artless,
I could not have resisted it—no, sir!)
A sallow guest drawn into chatter
Suddenly answered hotly, "The matter's
Rights. You talk so much of rights, now;
You ask so seldom what your duties are!
It used to be each knew
According to his stratum, the goodness required—
Though goodness knows goodness is foolhardy—
When there were strata—not one dull rock-bottom!—
Were—were—"

We knew those words, but did not speak to them,
And he saw it, worn-out friend:
As cups clicked and we began again,
Hastily snatching at the breach
(Sir, if that had been a passionate speech!)
My notion of what he was like,
My notion of what I was like,
The dark backyard of my understanding
Lit up, in a starfall on savagery.

36

I fell silent, eyes down. In a nightmare
I had strolled willy-nilly through my house
Turning on all the lights;
Touched, I waked cold—
                    The roaring sun was out.

# Illness

After supper for a breath of air
I went out on the front porch. God was there
Sitting on the top step smoking his pipe;
He had a white rag tied round his head,
And his aged eyes were running, unwiped.
"Oh, thank you," I cried suddenly free,
"It's been wonderful! this life." Eh? he said.
I had disturbed him somewhere other-orbited.
"This summer's shadows on the moss, daylilies rank—
The ivy, teal on Mrs. Reeves's pink wall—
But I forget—you conceive them from six feet tall?
And last winter—that day—
One, storm swathed trees; two, sun blazed; three, all day
About the lawn and in the trees, slash!
The storm stormed again, blinding exciting
Blind, and the branches ascended swirling?
And May—when the horse chestnuts were in bloom
We drove out the Coshocton Road
The horse chestnuts were just right
Just aesthetically right
Bouquets pinned on the hills over the lambs!
. . . . Then fall before last
The week the color was at its height—
God do you know Gambier Ohio?"
        You underestimate me, he smiled.
"And that's not all.
If I could tell you—
About my family!"
        It was not perfect, he sighed.
"Even being sick—three months, is it now?—
Wild to get up again and cast that aside—

I appreciate it."

        Good, he said wearily

And knocked his ashes in the petunia urn;
They fell into a fortune that read:
Fever, flesh, ash into ashes burn.

# Flesh and Spirit

You were like a strange older child, my sweet,
Strapping the hopeless skates on my lax feet;
When I came running forward for your hand,
Pushing me backward as a reprimand.
You handed me a paper love, attached
A kerosene ointment; you struck the match—
A blinding, deafening groan.
I wrapped my arms about myself.
"Stop!" you cried, this ruin saved for me alone.

When we were young, no history was lost;
Now not a day without ten riddles set
Of what I don't know, yet I can't forget:
My mother's voice blank as the day with frost,
Whether the winters were not harder then. . . .
Our feet were wrapped in tow sacks for the snow
(Don't touch! Don't take! Don't know!
Run out and play; come in.)—
After you I go, my life!
Was it chase or flight?

We were together then.
We dozed. The flying
Owls in the dark crying
Like scissors whacking the vegetation
To the side, to the front,
To here, to dream turns white—
"Dear dream, do not go," I cried.
Your outstretched hand replied
With the dazzling light.

Now I wait daily the day we part,
Cling, still unshed, rough shell of heart,
Like one awaked at night, too soon,
Clutching my foil pillow, abed in the moon.

# In the Churchyard

In the churchyard I hear them hammering
On the new roof of my new house
A hundred years old.
Cupped acorns glut the walks,
The greenish nuts crushed in.
Cupped earths hold up the bright memorial ferns.
They're gone!
Down over Mamma's face
They nailed, we nailed, I nailed the lid.
And there was Uncle Risdon.
Married a Miss Catherine Tye. Aunt Catherine
Somehow I can't now call her full name.
She took a galloping consumption
After she let the baby catch on fire.
Aunt Oratha despised the coat
That Uncle bought her. She died of pride.
Pride knoweth neither hot nor cold
But hers knew both.
They die of fleshly pride.
And Cousin Mazeppa took laudanum.
"Why did you do it, Zeppie, girl?
Wa'n't Daddy good to you?"
"Pray, let me sleep!"

Child, brave it to blind-out the fur
Of the evergreens in sun above:
They are too far;
Shade has rinsed out their sun,
Hushed up their green.
They'll dizzy one.

There's the rattat of the hammers—
The little nails, the little nails,
The birds eat out one's hands!

# Her Day

All day it had kept turning dark, like rain
Coming, or like the day of the eclipse,
When the cows had come up to the barn
And bellowed to be milked.
(If you could hear, for pain.)
They hadn't known. Was it the Second Coming?
    *No, Granny, dear, its not the end.*
They looked in the almanac, later on.

Now the cows were surely at the bars.
It was getting night, one might have known.
Some of you get a bucket and go on!
They prodded one another with their horns,
(If you could see, for pain.)
She sat up, fretted with a thread she'd torn.
They low so pitiful! Go on!
Gloom hushed her crying. She sank back, lost.
Presently her eyes fixed on the bedpost
And she chuckled softly.
Look a' that little nigger, laughin' at me!
Eyes closed. . . . Pneumonia, maybe. . . .
Pneumonia weather, we girls walked out for bluets, pinks,
What Ma called poison lilies, sprouting
From Back Bunn's meadow resurrectionwise
But with a sinful pink stain at the throat. . . .
As children we played down at Cluster Rocks,
On the river. Scary, it was—
We played clubfist—
Grab hold, Liza!

William Trembletoe
HE's a good fisherman
KETCHesiz his fish
putsum in the dish.

KETCHesiz his hens
putsum in the pens.
Some lay eggs
Some
don't
O,U,T, out, goes—if pain—

She gasped, You're choking, Wincie!
Made me cry, a grown woman
You play so mean, making grown women cry
Old women. . . . No, death choked
I'm there at last
I'll cross the golden river
The river that bright angel feet have trod
    (Does the river look muddled to you?
    There's no fishing in March;
    Wait till the water's clare.)
Then Cluster Rocks, alight, was here:
Behold! an old lady her uncles rowed across—
The boat beneath her slipped the bank
Just as she stepped ashore.
"Stretched me arightsmart," she chirped.
O to think of that dying!
O unworthy "Stretchedmearightsmart"!

She glared at hell through tears.

# Cursed

Life took me by the skinny-bones
And whirled me round and round and round;
My feet ached and my shirt came off
And when she put this burden down
It found that it was only fit for
Going round and round and round;
To hell tornadowise it went,
Then it was devil-backwards-sent
And put all heaven in torment
By throbbing round and round and round
Its balding head with skim of down,
Its veined feet and stomach bound
A little out from going round.
If it had only silent been!
But it had learned a word or two
And, as it shot from heaven down,
As it the fiery furnace flew,
Distracted both by murmuring,
*Bad cess to you! bad cess to you!*

# Madame

This is the sleep that fell just after dinner.

These are the windows that let in the sleep
That fell just after dinner.

This is the light that shed through the windows
That let in the sleep that fell just after dinner.

These are the lids that shut out the light
That shed through the windows
That let in the sleep that fell just after dinner.

These are the kisses the size of quarters that lay
On the lids that shut out the light that shed
Through the windows that let in the sleep
That fell just after dinner. . . .

Let us put them on her tray for a tip. . . .

    Oh, thank you, Madame!
    It was like you, to make life pleasant
    Somehow,
    Living or sleeping.

# Escape

At tidetime ocean mounts the earth
And bathers, magnified by dearth
Of beach, retire, wet-pouched,
Well-tamed, to screened porches.

One human form far out
Keeps on meeting the waves,
Back to them, face to them,
With a companion, no doubt;
A robot, perhaps, or a hypnotist?
From my poet's chair I watch, distressed—
Has she forgotten the tide today?
She can hardly swim, and won't cry out.
She slept late, I thought,
And stood, before the plunge,
Like one shedding not a towel
But a lifetime.
She has not moved, while others
Reminded of the distance back to earth,
Gave in.
Well, her hours have been with him!
Hypnotized, robotized,
The water pushes the mill wheel;
The wheel, wheeling, dispersing,
Disperses the starry spectacle
And drags the stone—
But what have inland veins to do with this?
There are companions and companions
There are times and times—She turns:
"No, no, just this
And how fragmentary it was! How stingy!
A shred each.
In two spots time and timelessness both live
Companions—
In art and death

Both oceans on my map—
And life forever mixing another drink—
Around, wheel!"

Now for a long time, where she was
Is all ocean.
I feel myself shouting.
Don't play with the ocean!
But there she is again,
For a tired moment she faces shore,
Then—turns her back forever on dabblers
As one who cries, Of course I meant it!
A vein of time gapes for her small transfusion.
There is a far white crash, too negligible to bear
And I sweep my eyes housekeeperly
With my hands—(forever!)
Hoping he knew he was there.

# Night

I spent the night in Chastelton.
The splitting damasks hung in belts;
Those faded colors we admired
Forgot themselves in gray.
Light spider-bagged the baseboards, tired.
I climbed up to the children's room.
I knew the way.
Up steps and past a blistered stile
Along that thick oak balustrade
(You like old things? Behold!)

The carved door hung ajar.
I pushed it wide.
The birds flew from their roosts
And disappeared like mice into the sky.
Below, the garden that one time
Held itself clipped urns, hens, cones,
Of evergreen, had turned
A calendar of wastes,
A zodiac of despairs.
There was somebody there.

It was you.
You were a mortal sheen
Flickering from the negative.
You were younger than last year,
Younger than the day we were married,
Younger than the day we met.
What are you doing?
To whom are you smiling?
Where are you going?
Will you not answer me?
Answer! Answer!

## Woman as Artist

I'm mother.
I hunt alone.
There is no bone
Too dry for me, mother,
Or too extra.

Have a care, boy.
The neat pearls nibbling at the chowder
Gently, with joy,
Contain powder.

> An emigrant from the mother tongue
> To say-so in the silent one,
> For me the stepped-for step sinks,
> The expected light winks
> Out; dear self, do not think
> On the ominous appetite rising insistently
> In the hour of no food. . . .
> Do not think of the mice in the clock
> When you start up in your sleeping hood.
> The light feathers of a year,
> Too fine to make a pillow,
> Not fine enough to wear
> Out anywhere, drop but like milk
> Into the snow
> Of what I say and bear.

Kneel, fathers.
If my babies are right,
It is not because of you!
Or me.
But I lick them dearly,
Scrutinize their toilette,
Every tendril pleasing
On account of me. . . .

Next year I'll dig them up
And separate them.
They'll multiply
    Multiply
        Multiply
Till the round earth's ringed with Babel trumpets,
Some dark, some light,
Some streakèdy.

When I first gave the question life,
The howling naked question life,
Did I not have some inkling of the answer,
And the answer answered,
The door that closed across the room
As my door opened?

In the morning, early,
Birds flew over the stable,
The morning glories ringed the flapping corn
With Saturn faces for the surly light,
And stars hung on the elder night.

But in the afternoon
Clouds came
Cyclonic gusts and chilling rain
Banged-to the windows of our heroine
Beginning to chronicle her wound-up skein.
Rib, spin.

# Romantic Abstract

Believe in me,
Who always meant to be.
I never can.
                    (I'm told
She slaps the baby's dirty hands,
The dishes mold.)

We were always apart in the dark
In deck chairs, shaking our heads
In vexation at our questions.
The light-tongued stars that spat the flower bed!
The mute, placed moon that stood stock dead!
The doctor would diagnose his soul:
Unreal, so, functional, he holds.

Does it matter whether it unlives at Anzio
Saving lives (mostly undertaking)
Or rotting as a yeasty testy case
(It nettled me to have them touch my dog
And say in their dispelling voices, *Dog*)
Or when the wifely salad hits your face?
                              (They tell me

She'll be found tippling
In the bright lonely rooms;
The receiver swings,
According to the laws of pendulums.)

You should have struck a light
In the dark I was, and
Said, Read, Be—be over!

We should have been leaning
Together over the window sill
Upstairs, watching the Milk Dipper
When the building fell.

That stricture in the upstairs throats
Would have been indeed the proper note.

But now no longer I, I will be she—
The one who didn't wait, but always does,
Who haunts your sickbed, fever-yearned:
She-just-she will hold her hand
Over the wound as you turn.

# Out of Habit

Plague take the way I call to mind
Things out of habit!
Cousin Risdon comes and sits
Against the window,
(I'd fear to see me better,
But he went blind at Argonne)
Refuses anything to drink,
(So I could fly out to the kitchen
For a minute, cry alone)
Puts his black bag at his feet
(Though actually he never reached med school—
That little pretense is so sweet).
I cry anyway, on my charm bracelet:
We were just the same age;
If I hadn't been a girl
I might have gone too. . . . Yes yes
I will dry up.
You don't mind if *I* smoke?
Remember reading Hambone in the swing?

But he desires to parley in black leather.
    Susan,
    The human eye is a wonderful thing.
    Through the lid, through sleep,
    We perceive day and wake.
    The eye accustoms itself to darkness,
    To delicate variations.
    After a number of years of darkness
    One might, suddenly, as seeds perceive,
    Perceive the light, sifting like rainfall,
    Like the sun drawing water,
    Through the porous earth
    To our soft coffins—
    For light does penetrate
    Cloud, night,

Lids, sleep,
Earth—
Why not death?

# Song

Oh my dearie,
Our childhoods are histories,
Buckets at the bottom of the well,
And hard to tell
Whether they will hold water or no.
Did Pa die before we were married?
No, he died in twenty-seven,
But I remember the wedding
Reminded me of the funeral—
When the grandbabies ask,
Little do they care,
I will tell them about the man I found
That day at my plowing in the low-grounds
Lying at the edge of the water.
His face had bathed five nights.
A dark man, a foreigner, like.
They never found his kin to tell. . . .
Buckets, buckets at the bottom of the well.
It was in the paper with my name.
I found him.
I have the clipping tells all about it,
If your Grandma aint thrown it out.

Oh my dearie
When our faces are swol up
We will look strange to them.
Nobody, looking out the door
Will think to call us in.
They'll snap their fingers trying
To recollect our names.
Five nights, five bones, five buckets—
Who'll ever hear a sound?
Oh my dearie
The rope broke
The bucket bobs round
Oh my dearie

# My Grandmother's Virginhood, 1870

When I disrobed to go to bed
It seemed to me like something said:
Hold your shimmy round you tight—
Somebody may be around tonight—
Aint no curtain, aint no shade—
Don't hurt none to be afraid—
    Little David McSwain!

Walked us both home from the dance
Wearing new black homespun pants.
When we got up to the door
Catched us both around the waist
And—kissed us! Lor!
What's he getting—kisses! from us for?
    Little David McSwain!

## Motherhood, 1880

When Dave got up and struck a light
We'd neither of us slept all night.
We kept the fire and watched by May,
Sick for fear she might
Go off like little Tom. . . . They say
"Don't fret . . . another on the way. . . ."
They know I favor this least child.

No use to cry. But while
I made a fire in the kitchen stove
I heard a pesky mourning dove.
Lor! What's he calling "O-love" for?

# Family Bible

## 1. Uncle

Typical of the presents
Grandma gave Grandpa
Was Uncle Mun,
A baroque buckle
Not to be undone.
He thought before he spoke,
Abstained from drink, snuff, smoke,
Marriage; ate and dressed frugally,
Reproved respectfully
His mother's yen
For jet beads on her birthday.
Was it not thoughtful of him
On her busy death day
As she counted quilt-blocks
To elicit this data
In Spencerian pencil
Laid away in the clock
For me,
Posterity?
    My full name is Aminta Dunlap Watkins Ross.
    My mother was Merina Wilkerson.
    My father was Arnold Watkins—he carpentered—
    I married your pa Whitson Ross
    My wedding presents were a feather bed and two hens.

## 2. Grandmother

The hens gone on the honeymooning coach,
Squawking and scratching at the black hope chest;
She made her bed and it was hard, for rest
Too hard; when broken dreams and sleep encroached
Upon stark wakefulness, she walked the stars;
Her unread eye imagined what they meant:
Job's Coffin and the Seven Sisters, the fine-print

Groups; then what said those blazing sky-far,
A sky not like a page, a script not like a word,
But taking or leaving a star,
A world, as it just chose?
How the hymn book puzzled her,
Singing "Jesus and Shall"—
And the notes of the music,
If one read, like the choir!
*'Tis midnight in my soul till He*
*Bright morning Star! bid darkness flee.*


### 3. Grandfather

The fear of hell was all,
His children wheezed,
That wore Whit Ross's pants
Out at the knees.
His poverty enraged him
(A hoe
To cultivate flint rocks,
Breeches to thwart the briers)
His wits fanned up his ignorance
Like a fire.
Something savage in him
Fought civility.
If he had but been born nobility!
Beaten sexless lifeless
Souls touched him.
When a black boy Joe died—
What had he ever had
From life to give to death?
He found a far-off part
Of meadow land
To cry his tears.
"A Christian spirit needs

Not cherry bounce,
Mint, be a good woman—
The Bible says!"


4. Grandparents

The Bible says!
The Bible looked not right to her.
It should be short, straight rules,
Not run-on continuities the stops left out
So hard to read for true.
The Bible says!
She wept before the finger.
She sought out her eldest son
In the middle of the day.
"Boy, pray for me."
His coattails, her calico black skirts
Puddled about the shoes and knees.
Was it forgiven? It was gone,
The heathen dancing
With her giggling sisters;
They flew about the room
In seedstitch weskits
Like eight wax dolls gone flaskwards.
Those were gay days!
She sighed a mournful tune
Waddling about her everyday
Affairs of life and death
(Affairs of painful life, uncertain death):
"Wild loneliness that beats
Its wings on life," she sang.
She thwacked a pone in two,
Her big hand for a knife.
Thar! stirring it severely,
And thar! into the oven . . .

'Twould be wormwood and ashes.
A spray of peacock feathers
Begged from her father's house
Splattered the dining room wall.
(She pretended to Whit
That she dusted with it.)
The table was small for nine;
The honeycomb, buttered,
Hived in glass vines.

## 5. Granddaughter

When she was old, deaf, widowed, my grandmother,
She came to spend a lonely night at home.
When I went to call her in to breakfast
She did not hear my brave voice for her comb
Running through her hair in little flights—
(Long, long hair as much gold as white,
Flying with old-fashioned electricity
From the comb's old-fashioned friction)
And as she rocked, her shell-combs on her knee,
Suddenly aware, she looked up at me
Through her shimmering hair, startled, and smiled.
Air ye awake, little gal?
Perhaps she thought I was admiring her.
She gave a proud, delighted, sidewise smile
Flashing her small gray teeth and elf-arched eyes,
For a ninety-eight-point-six degrees' response.
But she was disappointed, though I smiled.
Her silent island threatened me enchantment;
The joints too lithe to creak when I bent over
Sailed off without retrieving for her
A big bone hairpin wrecked upon the floor.

The day she was buried
I played sick and lay abed

Claiming fever.
I did not see her dead.
But eight months before
At Rehobath Church
On Homecoming Day
I stood with a crowd
Of boys and girls, and
Watched her cross the churchyard
Slowly, alone; from end to end
She crossed the yard,
Her head thrown back,
Swathed deep in black—
Long skirts, pointed black toes,
The wind parting her many veils,
The blue eyes beneath roving, veiled—
And leaning on a stick.
She seemed a giant Figure,
All eyes upon her;
Yet none spoke.
And all my heart said,
Run to her! Claim her!
(Wild loneliness that
Beats its wings on death)
Then the spell broke.
We who had waved across so many chasms
No longer had to say we were not close.
Was closeness more than painful separateness?
We were a constellation of detached, like, ghosts.